THE COMPLETE GUIDE TO COPYWRITING

CRAFTING COMPELLING COPY

SAMYAK RAMTEKE

Contents

CHAPTER ONE

INTRODUCTION

Copywriting is one of the most essential elements of effective online marketing.

The art and science of direct-response copywriting involves strategically delivering words (whether written or spoken) which get people to take some form of action.

Copywriters are some of the highest-paid writers in the world, but to become a truly proficient and profitable copy expert, you'll need to invest time and energy in studying the craft.

Ready to get started?

Let take a peek behind the curtain, and discover the real "secrets" to improving your copywriting skills.

CHAPTER TWO

FUNDAMENTALS OF COPYWRITING

What Is Copywriting?

Copywriting is the practice of crafting written text in order to inform, inspire or persuade. Copywriting consists of the words, either written or spoken, marketers use to try to get people to take an action after reading or hearing them. In most cases, copywriting is used to increase sales and conversions.

Mediums, where copywriting is implemented, include sales letters, blog posts, advertisements and social media posts.

Why Is Copywriting Important?

In this age of video and podcasts, does copywriting still matter?

In a word: yes.

Here are some of the benefits that you can get from becoming good at copywriting:

- Get higher conversion rates on key pages
- Improve structure and flow of articles
- Get more engagement on social media posts
- Have more people share your content
- Understand your customer's needs and wants

In other words: copywriting can improve nearly every element of your marketing.

This obviously includes articles and sales pages. But copywriting also comes into play when creating:

- Video scripts
- Blog post headlines
- Webpage meta descriptions
- Outreach emails
- YouTube video descriptions
- Podcast descriptions
- Interview questions
- Facebook posts
- Press releases
- About page copy

Goal of a Copywriting is to

- Inform
- Inspire
- Persuade people into taking action
- Develop your brand voice
- Get sales

What Does a Copywriter Do?

Needless to say, a copywriter spends most of his or her day writing. However, there's more to a copywriter's job than putting words after words.

In fact, experienced copywriters spend significant amounts of time learning about their customers. They also invest time in understanding how the product they're writing about can help their prospects.

If you're writing copy for your own product or service then you probably already know what it is, how it works, and how it compares to the competition. So your job is to learn about your audience's thoughts, fears and desires. And how they phrase these things in their mind. That way, you can write copy that speaks directly to them.

How To Become a Copywriter

Fortunately, you don't need any formal training or education to become a copywriter. Instead, you need to get good at the following skills:

- Customer research
- Sentence structure
- Web copywriting
- Grammar and spelling
- Persuasion
- Content structure
- Online advertising

To be clear: becoming a good copywriter takes time. But it's a marketing skill that you can use to get clients as a freelance copywriter or to improve your job prospects.

CHAPTER THREE

How to Write Amazing Headlines

You've probably heard the old adage: "80% of people read the headline, and only 20% read the copy."

Is that number accurate? Who knows!

But what I do know is that your headline is SUPER important.

Fortunately, writing awesome headlines isn't as hard as you might think.

All you need to do is follow the simple techniques in this chapter.

Be Insanely Specific

Your headline needs to be insanely specific.

Why?

Because specificity sells.

In other words:

Your headline should tell your prospect EXACTLY what they're gonna get.

For example, if a blogpost headline is

> "*"Save More Time The Easy Way".*"

It's not horrible. But not nearly specific enough.

But if you write something like

> "*"Save 2 Hours Per Day With These 7 Productivity Hacks".*"

Look at how much better this super-specific headline sounds:

And this rule doesn't just apply to blog content.

For example, Snap.hr cites a specific timeframe for getting a result:

> "*"Hire your next developer, designer, date scientist or product manager in 14 days"*"

Blanco

Use a Number

Replace adjectives with specific data.

- "Less time" → "24 hours less".
- "Lots of nutrients" → "23 essential nutrients".
- "More conversions" → "2x increase in conversions".

Numbers FORCE you to write insanely specific headlines.

For example, look at what happens when you take this bland headline...

"*"Connect With The World's Best Designers"*"

...and add a number to it:

Get Your Project in Front of 60,627 World-Class Designers"

It's MUCH more compelling... and specific.

Strong Emotions

The best headlines tend to be emotional headlines.

The question is:

How do you create emotional headlines?

First, add emotionally-charged words to your headline copy.

Here are a few examples:

- Crazy
- Now
- Fast
- Mistake
- New
- Breakthrough
- Amazing

Obviously, you don't want to go overboard.

No one's going to believe a headline like "New Crazy Amazing Breakthrough That Works Fast!"

But adding one or two of these words to your headline can make it more compelling:

"*25 AWESOME Email Marketing Tools*"

Second, analyze your headline with a tool like the American Marketing Institute Headline Analyzer. This tool will analyze your headline to determine the Emotional Marketing Value (EMV) score based on proprietary analysis technology.

And it will give you a score from 0-100%.

I try to get my headlines to at least 30%... especially for sales pages and landing pages.

Use The Four U's

The copywriting trainers at American Writers & Artists teach The Four U's approach to writing headlines.

Headlines, subheads and bullets should:

- Be USEFUL to the reader,
- Provide him with a sense of URGENCY,
- Convey the idea that the main benefit is somehow UNIQUE; and
- Do all of the above in an ULTRA-SPECIFIC way.

Copywriter Clayton Makepeace says to ask yourself six questions before you start to write your headline:

- Does your headline offer the reader a reward for reading?
- What specifics could you add to make your headline more intriguing and believable?
- Does your headline trigger a strong, actionable emotion the reader already has about the subject at hand?
- Does your headline present a proposition that will instantly get your prospect nodding his or her head?

- Could your headline benefit from the inclusion of a proposed transaction?
- Could you add an element of intrigue to drive the prospect into your opening copy?

Makepeace's six questions combined with the basic structure of The Four U's provide an excellent framework for writing spectacular headlines. Note that just about any headline which satisfies the framework will fall into one of the eight categories you learned in the last section.

It takes work and focus, but the effort will make you a more popular blogger and a more profitable businessperson.

Use FOMO

FOMO can make your headlines 10x more powerful.

That said:

FOMO (Fear of Missing Out) doesn't work for every situation.

But if you can use FOMO you should use FOMO.

That's because FOMO triggers a strong emotion in your prospects...

...an emotion that makes them want to hear what you have to say.

Answer: What's in it for me?

Let me know if this sounds familiar:

You land on a site.

And the first thing you see is a headline that's all about THEM.

> "*"We've been a Leader in the SEO Space for 20 Years"*"

Who. The heck. CARES.

Instead, you want to write headlines that are all about your customer.

In other words, your headline should answer the question in your customer's mind:

"What's in it for me?"

For example, this homepage headline is:

> "*Emails campaigns that run your entire Shopify store*"

Is the headline fancy?

Nope.

But if you're looking to grow your Shopify store, this headline lets you know that you're in the right place.

CHAPTER FOUR

The Structure of Persuasive Copy

Good content structure is never written in stone, but persuasive copy will do certain things and contain certain elements time and time again.

Whether you're writing a sales page, long blog post, or promotional ebook, the flow will determine effectiveness. Here are some guidelines:

- First of all, focus on the reader – make an important promise early on (with your headline and opening paragraphs) that tells the reader what's in it for her. Never allow readers to question why they are bothering to pay attention.
- Each separate part of your narrative should have a main idea (something compelling) and a main purpose (to rile up the reader, to counter an opposing view, etc) which supports your bigger point and promise. Don't digress, and don't ramble. Stay laser focused.

- Be ultra-specific in your assertions, and always make sure to give "reasons why." General statements which are unsupported by specific facts cause a reader's BS detector to go on high alert.
- Demonstrate large amounts of credibility, using statistics, expert references, and testimonials as appropriate. You must be authoritative—if you're not an existing expert on a subject, you'd better have done your research.
- After building your credibility and authority, make sure you get back to the most important person — the reader. What's STILL in it for him? Restate the hook and the promise that got readers engaged in the first place.
- Make an offer. Whether you're selling a product or selling an idea, you've got to explicitly present it for acceptance by the reader. Be bold and firm when you present your offer, and relieve the reader's risk of acceptance by standing behind what you say.
- Sum everything up, returning full circle to your original promise and demonstrate how you've fulfilled it.
- These are some of the key elements of persuasive copy. Use them to provide a "roadmap" to your writing, and you'll achieve better results.

Your copy is intriguing once the average reader effortlessly makes it to the end. A hook, peak, and satisfying ending are your trifecta of intrigue.

CHAPTER FIVE

MASTER THE LEAD

The lead is VERY underrated.

In my experience, your lead is just as important as your headline.

That's because your prospect uses the first few lines of your copy to decide whether or not to keep reading. And if you lose them here, you've lost them for good.

With that, here are simple strategies that you can use to write compelling leads.

Start With a Hook

The first sentence of your lead is HUGE.

So make sure your first line grabs people by the eyeballs.

For example, this lead from one of our sales pages is designed to grab attention with a compelling stat:

> "*"I recently published a blog post that brought in 50,384 visits in 7 days."*"

And here are some "copy and paste" first lines that you can use in your leads:

- "Does this sound familiar?"
- "Now you can now [benefit] in [timeframe] without [common solution]"
- "You know the feeling..."
- "New study finds [surprising result]"
- "Introducing: [product name]. A new way to [benefit] backed by [proof]"
- "I struggled with [problem] for [X years]. Until one day..."

Use Mini-Stories

Stories are a great way to hook people... and keep them reading.

The problem is:

Your lead should be short and sweet. This means you don't have a lot of room to tell an epic story.

Enter: Mini-stories.

As the name suggests, mini-stories condense a story into 4-5 lines.

Complement the Headline

Sometimes your lead can just complement your headline.

In other words, you use your headline to grab their attention:

And drum up interest with your lead:

(Yup, that's the "A" and "I" from the AIDA Formula.)

8 Lines or Less

Whether it's a blog post, video script, sales page or email newsletter, you want your lead to be SUPER short.

(8 lines max.)

Remember:

The goal of your lead is to grab someone's attention so they keep reading.

And once you've done that, it's time to transition into the meat of your page.

That way, I hook the reader with a strong lead... then jump right into the content itself.

> "*Your writing is succinct once everything unimportant is removed.*"

CHAPTER SIX

WRITE A COMPELLING COPY

"A sentence should contain no unnecessary words, a paragraph no unnecessary sentences, for the same reason that a drawing should have no unnecessary lines and a machine no unnecessary parts. This requires not that the writer make all his sentences short, or that he avoid all detail and treat his subjects only in outline, but that every word tell."

—The Elements of Style by Strunk & White.

Blanco

Write Like You Talk

This is the ultimate copywriting superhack.

The best way to do this is to read all of your copy out loud.

If it sounds weird, rewrite it.

But if your copy sounds good out loud, You know it's good to go.

Short Sentences

Short sentences+better copy.

The longer the sentence, the shorter the reading comprehension.

Bottom line?

Use short sentences. They're easy to read AND understand.

Write to one person

In other words, AVOID copy like this:

> "*"Lots of people struggle with weight loss. They've tried diets. They've tried exercise. But nothing seems to work."*"

Instead, write to one person:

> "*"If you're reading this it means that you're struggling to lose weight. You tried diets. You tried exercise. But nothing seems to work."*"

This also applies to B2B.

B2B copywriters LOVE to write copy that speaks to absolutely no one.

Here's an example:

> "*"ABC Company helps small business get more by building online presence. Businesses trust ABC because our proprietary systems are the best in the industry."*"

And here's an example of B2B copy that speaks directly to the reader:

> "*"Want to build an online presence? Then the ABC Company is for you. We've helped small business owners like you to increase their online presence by 25%"*"

Blanco

Entice with Benefits, Not Features

Your customers never buy the product, they buy the results.

Be specific with the benefits by tying them with one of the features of the product.

Think to yourself: "What problem does my customer need solved?"

Don't Create Fake Benefits

The idea of highlighting benefits over features seems simple. But it's often tough to do in practice.

Writers often end up with fake benefits instead.

Top copywriter Clayton Makepeace asserts that fake benefits will kill sales copy, so you have to be on the lookout for them in your writing. He uses this headline as an example: "Balance Blood Sugar Levels Naturally!"

That sounds pretty beneficial, doesn't it? In reality, there's not a single real benefit in the headline.

Create True Benefits

Makepeace advises to apply his patented "forehead slap" test to see if your copy truly contains a benefit to the reader. In other words, have you ever woken up from a deep sleep, slapped yourself in the forehead, and exclaimed "Man... I need to balance my blood sugar levels naturally!"

It doesn't happen. So getting someone to pull out their wallet to buy that so-called "benefit" will be difficult at best.

Here's how Makepeace identifies the real benefit hidden in that headline:

Nobody really wants to balance their blood sugar levels. But anyone in his or her right mind DOES want to avoid the misery of blindness ... cold, numb, painful limbs ... amputation ... and premature death that go along with diabetes.

A high risk person will want to avoid the terrible effects of diabetes. That is the true benefit that the example product offers.

How to Extract True Benefits

So, how do you successfully extract true benefits from features? Here's a four-step process that works:

- First, make a list of every feature of your product or service.
- Second, ask yourself why each feature is included in the first place.
- Third, take the "why" and ask "how" does this connect with the prospect's desires?

- Fourth, get to the absolute root of what's in it for the prospect at an emotional level.

Let's look at a product feature for a fictional News Feed Reader app: Feature:

> “*“Contains an artificial intelligence algorithm.”*”

Why it's there:

> “*“Adds greater utility by adapting and customizing the user's information experience.”*”

What's in it for them:

> “*“Keeps the things you read the most at the forefront when you're in a hurry.”*”

Emotional Root:

> “*“Stay up to date on the things that add value to your life and career, without getting stressed out from information overload.”*”

Getting to the emotional root is crucial for effective consumer sales. But what about business prospects?

When Features Work

When a feature is fairly well known and expected from your audience, you don't need to sell it.

However, with innovative features, you still need to move the prospect down the four-step path.

While the phrase "contains an artificial intelligence algorithm" may be enough to get the Slashdot reader salivating, he'll still want to know how it works and what it does for him. The What's in it for me? aspect remains crucial.

Sell With Benefits, Support With Features

We're not as logical as we'd like to think we are. Most of our decisions are based on deep-rooted emotional motivations, which we then justify with logical processes. So, first help the right brain create desire, then satisfy the left brain with features and hard data so that the wallet actually emerges.

Persuading your reader with features and benefits is important -- but you also need to know how to craft a truly compelling offer.

Active Voice

Look at these two lines:

Passive Voice:

The blog post was written by Samyak.

Active Voice:

Samyak wrote a blog post.

As you can see, the active voice sounds MUCH better.

You can check the active vs. passive voice with a tool like Hemingway.com.

No Big Words

Big words don't impress anyone.

In fact, they make your copy hard to read.

And as I like to say:

Hard to read = won't read.

So avoid fancy words like these:

- Utilize
- Overwrought
- Fascinating
- Conscientious
- Unparalleled
- Demonstrates

You get the idea.

Instead, stick to terms that are easy to read and understand, like:

- Use
- Excited
- Interesting
- Notice
- Unique
- Show

Write For Skimmers

Here's a good rule to follow for ALL of the content marketing that you do:

People online don't read. They skim.

That's why you want to format your copy for skimmers.

Here's how:

First, use lots of subheadings.

These break up your content into little chunks.

This post is 3,759 words.

Write with nouns and verbs

Precise language convinces; flowery language distracts. Concise and specific copy moves the prospect along, but adjectives and adverbs are (often) just filler. The more descriptors you throw in there, the higher the chances are that someone with the attention span of a hummingbird will click away (unless you are describing the features of something technical).

Make an Offer

It's troubling to see so many entities trying to gain business online, yet without ever making a compelling offer.

There's no apparent reason why someone should select you from the overcrowded field, because often you've made no express offer at all.

So many websites assume that a visitor will get the obvious value that the owner knows he provides.

Value is communicated through offers, however, and those offers must be communicated quickly and explicitly.

Consider your own surfing habits for a second, and ask yourself – why would my target audience be any different?

In the lingo of direct-response copywriting, an offer is a call to action.

For bloggers, desired actions include having a reader subscribe, bookmark you, make comments, respond to surveys, share your post on social networking sites, and utilize your information resources that double as sales tools.

Start making offers if you want some action.

CHAPTER SEVEN

Pro Copywriting Strategies

This chapter is a list of 6 copywriting strategies that you can use to write better copy from scratch...

...or improve your existing copy.

So if you want actionable copywriting tips that you can implement the right way, this chapter is for you.

The "AIDA" Formula

AIDA is a powerful copywriting formula that works for:

- Sales pages
- Squeeze pages
- Blog post intros
- Email newsletters
- Video scripts
- And more

As you can see, AIDA stands for:

Attention.

Interest.

Desire.

Action.

First, grab attention with the first line.

Then, drum up interest with a blod promise.

And tap into the #1 desire

Then, give readers a call to action that pushes them to keep things interesting.

Benefits > Features

The features are nice.

But benefits sell.

For example, let's say you just launched a new piece of software designed to help people become more productive.

Strong CTAs

A strong call-to-action is the difference between a page that converts... and one that falls flat.

Seriously.

Here's why your CTA is so important:

Your prospect is busy. VERY busy.

Which means they don't have time to figure out what they're supposed to do next.

So tell them exactly what to do.

Social Proof

Social proof is important when someone's deciding whether or not to buy what you sell.

That's why pro copywriters PACK their copy with results, case studies and testimonials.

How to Solve The "Social Proof Paradox"

You need social proof to sell. But you need sales to get social proof.

I call this "The Social Proof Paradox". And it's a real challenge.

Fortunately, there's an easy way to sidestep this problem:

Feature your strongest form of social proof.

Crystal Clear USP

USP=Unique Selling Proposition.

In other words, here's where you answer the question:

"Why should someone buy from YOU?".

Maybe you've got the best prices.

Maybe you deliver faster than anyone else.

Or maybe you guarantee results.

Either way, your copy needs to scream your USP at the top of its lungs.

And if you don't have a USP?

Well, you've got bigger problems than copywriting. But that's another story...

Sense of Urgency

How do you get customers to buy NOW?

Urgency.

Here are some easy ways to create a sense of urgency in your copy:

- "Limited time offer"
- "Quantities limited"
- "Only 47 left"
- "Sale ends on August 31st"
- "Doors close on Thursday"
- "Don't miss out"

(Needless to say, these statements should be backed up with real limitations. Otherwise, you'll lose people's trust.)

CHAPTER EIGHT

Advanced Copywriting Strategies

We covered the basics.

And now it's time to develop some advanced copywriting skills.

In this chapter, I'm going to transition into more advanced copywriting strategies and approaches.

So without further ado, let's get started.

Use "Crooked Numbers"

"Crooked Numbers" are numbers that aren't rounded.

For example:

- 57
- 8,913
- 41.9%
- 12.4

As it turns out, crooked numbers are more believable than round numbers.

That's why you DON'T want to round numbers in your copy.

For example, check out the intro from one of my recent blog posts:

I could have rounded up my monthly traffic to something like "over 500,000".

But I went with the exact number:

Don't talk about your product.

Instead, Show people what it can do.

Letting users know how your product works can help them inform as well as promote your product to their friends.

Use Clear Button Copy

Most people put zero thought into their button copy.

And it's a big mistake.

Why?

Because clicking a button is usually the last step for any conversion on a website.

With that, here's how to write high-converting button copy:

Make the outcome crystal clear.

Reduce Price Objections

Here's how this works:

A few years ago researchers at the University of Pittsburgh looked at how the wording of a mandatory fee affected conversions.

One group saw an overnight delivery fee described as:

"$5 fee"

And another saw the same fee described as:

"A small $5 fee"

Amazingly, the conversion rate of the "A small $5 fee" group was 20% higher than the group that read about the "$5 fee".

In other words:

Adding the term "a small" made a HUGE dent in conversions.

How can you use this research in your own copy?

Well, let's say you have a fee or charge that you want to minimize.

Use terms that make them seem small and insignificant.

And you might just notice conversions boost.

Make Your Testimonials 10x More Effective

According to Bigcommerce, customer testimonials and case studies can boost sales by 62%.

That is if you use them right.

Unfortunately, most testimonials look very bland. It doesn't push you to buy.

Instead, you want your testimonials to follow this proven formula:

First, you have the Before.

Here's where your customer paints a picture of where they were BEFORE they tried your product.

That way, your testimonial is SUPER relatable.

Next, you have After.

This is a set of specific results that your customer got from your product.

Finally, you have "What They'd Tell Someone".

Here's where you ask your customer: "What would you tell someone that's considering this product".

Dissect good copywriting

To learn what a job well done looks like, dissect your favorite copy's: highlight the best and worst parts of each and identify what makes them so.

CHAPTER NINE

More Tips to Help You Become a Better Copywriter

- Copywriting is 80% research, 15% editing and 5% writing.
- Write fast, edit slow.
- Use “you” 5x more than “I”.
- Always focus on 1 problem, 1 emotion, 1 solution.
- Only writing about the benefits and not explaining the features will make you sound like a snakeoil salesman.
- Don’t fake testimonials, people can sniff them out.
- No-one will read your CTA if your hook sucks.
- Never start writing from the hook.
- Copywriting is more about psychology and less about writing.
- Starting sentences with “but” can make your previous claim weaker.

- People don't read the titles of scientific studies, a long citation is enough to build authority.
- Alliteration – or starting every word with the same letter – is a powerful way to be memorable.
- It's not about how you write, it's what you write about.
- Never put the CTA under the hook on a sales page.
- Even the world's best copywriters don't 'know' what will convert the best, only testing will show you.
- Use the jargon your target audience uses.
- Drop the copywriting book and pick up the pen.
- Get people to say "yes" throughout your copy.
- Commas can make your writing lose its flow.
- Record yourself reading the copy to realize where it doesn't flow.
- Ask "So what?" after every sentence you write.
- Break your paragraphs into smaller pieces.
- Build a Copwriting checklist
    - Before writing:
        - define buyer awareness
        - research statistics
        - define buyer goals
        - define current buyer situation
    - During:
        - transition words
        - include stats when possible
        - shine a light on your solution
    - After:

- cut out fluff
- read out loud

Now it's Your Turn

I hope you enjoyed my ultimate guide to copywriting.

Pick up a pen and start writing.

9 798886 679038

Printed by Libri Plureos GmbH in Hamburg, Germany